MASTER DRAWINGS
The Art Institute of Chicago

Master Drawings
from
The Art Institute of Chicago

An Exhibition held at Wildenstein
19 East 64th Street, New York

October 17th through November 30th, 1963

The proceeds from this Exhibition will be used to establish a research fund
in the Department of Prints and Drawings of The Art Institute of Chicago.

Illustrated on the cover:
No. 5. Veronese: Head of a Woman
GIFT
Library of Congress Catalog Card Number: 63-20980
Manufactured in the U.S.A. by R.R. Donnelley & Sons Company
Design: Suzette M. Zurcher

Foreword

That The Art Institute of Chicago is engaged in forming a collection of drawings to be worthy of its famous collection of paintings, is hardly news in New York art circles. On numerous occasions, drawings from the Institute have played an important part in exhibitions such as *Drawings by Rembrandt* at the Morgan Library, *Cézanne, Gauguin,* and *French Drawings from American Collections* at the Metropolitan Museum, *Redon, Rodin, Toulouse-Lautrec,* and *Picasso* at The Museum of Modern Art. But the full range of the collection could only be appreciated by those who saw it in Chicago. For this reason, the Trustees of The Art Institute of Chicago accepted with pleasure the invitation of Messrs. Wildenstein and Company to exhibit a selected group of drawings in the galleries of their firm, which through many years has supplied the Art Institute with an impressive number of masterpieces. The pleasure, however, is tempered by deep sorrow over the untimely death of Georges Wildenstein, who looked upon this project with warm sympathy. We should like to take this occasion to pay tribute to a distinguished man who in his rare combination of scholarship and connoisseurship cannot be replaced in our time.

The international reputation of the Art Institute rests primarily on its collection of nineteenth century French paintings, the largest part of which had been donated in the nineteen-twenties and -thirties. At that time, there was but one member of the Board of Trustees, Robert Allerton (now Honorary President of the Art Institute), who thought there should be a collection of drawings worthy of the paintings, and it was through his generosity and foresight that the Institute, from 1922 onward, gained its first drawings by Ingres, Daumier, Degas, Renoir, Van Gogh, Seurat, and Picasso, to mention but a few. Mr. Allerton's pioneering effort was not in vain: Daniel Catton Rich, who in 1939 became Director of Fine Arts, took up the challenge and, in 1940, gained in Carl O. Schniewind an eminent curator who knew and loved drawings and who, moreover, had the rare talent for imparting his enthusiasm to others. Due to wartime conditions, at first, the going was rough, but in 1944 Mrs. Tiffany Blake decided to support Mr. Schniewind in the quest for distinguished drawings, and this marked the beginning of a period in which the collection grew immensely, more in quality and importance than in actual quantity. Rembrandt and Watteau were added to the roster of artists with examples of the highest order. One important point, upon which Mrs. Blake and Carl Schniewind agreed from the very start, was to acquire a drawing because of its intrinsic merit, not because of the name attached.

Fortunately for the Art Institute, Mrs. Blake's generous and warm interest in the collection has not diminished after Carl Schniewind's tragic death in 1957. In recent years, since 1958, the collection has also been immeasurably enriched by the many distinguished gifts of Mrs. Joseph Regenstein, among them drawings which have never been published before, such as the two marvelous sheets by Magnasco and the Neapolitan park scene by Fragonard. Unhappily, space does not permit us to name here all the generous friends of the Art Institute who helped to make the collection what it is today. But mention must be made of the fact that the department could not have flourished without the energetic, self-effacing support it has received since 1947 from its chairman, Frank B. Hubachek.

A collection of drawings in a great museum may fulfill two different functions. It can and must support the existing collection of paintings in its strong areas, and it can also capture the spirit of eras which are weakly represented by paintings, especially because there is little hope today for correcting the latter situation. Thus, it was natural that our drawing collection should stress nineteenth century France, but as the Institute's painting collection is weak in eighteenth century France, drawings could admirably fill that gap, the more so as within the life work of such leading figures as Watteau, Boucher, and Fragonard, drawing occupied an autonomous position by no means inferior to painting.

As we go further back past the year 1700, the coherence, which characterizes the eighteenth and nineteenth century group, no longer prevails. This is the inevitable weakness of a young collection. The Institute has no Leonardo, Raphael, Michelangelo, nor Dürer; but this is not to say that it has neglected the earlier centuries. There is a large group of drawings, mainly Italian, from the later sixteenth and the seventeenth century, known as the Leonora Hall Gurley Collection, which contains much interesting and challenging material for the serious student; and only recently, highly important drawings by Pisanello and Carpaccio, for example, have been added.

The selection made for this exhibition does not strive for historical balance, but rather tries to underscore the unique character of the collection, which lies in its consistency in the field of eighteenth and nineteenth century French drawings. To achieve this, other areas and countries had to be curtailed. The range of the exhibition could best be described by borrowing the title of a superb book by Jakob Rosenberg: "Great Draughtsmen from Pisanello to Picasso." As our Pisanello can firmly be dated 1438, and one of our Picassos bears the year 1944, this means a span of more than five hundred years. Since one has to stop at some point, it was decided not to include artists born after 1900, even though the collection contains many works by younger artists.

It is a pleasant duty to thank Mrs. David Fryberger and Gordon Hueter, staff members of the Department of Prints and Drawings, who gave their untiring assistance in the preparation of the exhibition. Mr. Hueter also made many of the "French" mats which, for some of us, are so preferable to the surgical white mats commonly used. We also wish to express our appreciation to William McCormick Blair, President of the Art Institute, and to Allan McNab, Director of Administration, for their effective help in organizing this exhibition, and to Mrs. Suzette Morton Zurcher for her catalogue design.

John Maxon, Director of Fine Arts   Harold Joachim, Curator of Prints and Drawings

Catalogue

The term drawing *is used in this catalogue in its widest possible application: as art on paper, including water colors and pastels, but excluding prints. Measurements are given in millimeters and inches. In both cases, height precedes width. Where the artist has inscribed the date on his work, the fact is indicated in the title entry by enclosing the date of execution in quotes.*

Italy before 1800

ANONYMOUS NORTH ITALIAN 15th Century
1   Portrait of a Young Priest   (Pl. I)
Silverpoint. 250 x 175 mm. 9¾ x 6⅞ in.
Gift of Tiffany and Margaret Blake   57.59

ANTONIO PISANO called PISANELLO   ca. 1395–1455
2   Studies of the Patriarch of Constantinople.   1438   (Pl. III)
verso: Studies of Quivers, Bow and Arrows
Pen and ink. 190 x 263 mm. 7½ x 10⅜ in.
Gift of Tiffany and Margaret Blake   61.331

FRA BARTOLOMMEO   1472–1517
3   Hermitage on the Slope of a Hill
verso: Watermill
Pen and ink. 290 x 215 mm. 11½ x 8½ in.
The Clarence Buckingham Collection   57.530

VITTORE CARPACCIO   first mentioned 1472;   died 1525
4   Two Kneeling Ecclesiastics
verso: Standing Youth   (Pl. II)
Brush in grey and white on blue-green paper. 195 x 253 mm. 7⅝ x 10 in.
The Joseph and Helen Regenstein Collection   62.577

PAOLO CALIARI called VERONESE   ca. 1530–1588
5   Head of a Woman (Cover illustration)
Black and white chalk on blue paper. 267 x 185 mm. 10½ x 7¼ in.
Gift of Tiffany and Margaret Blake   62.809

6   Studies for a Descent from the Cross   (Pl. V)
Pen and wash. 283 x 207 mm. 11⅛ x 8⅛ in.
The Robert Alexander Waller Memorial Fund   43.1060

JACOPO PALMA called IL GIOVANE   1544–1628
7   The Entombment   (Pl. IV)
Pen and wash heightened with gold on grey-green paper
223 x 140 mm. 8¾ x 5½ in.
The Clarence Buckingham Collection   62.376

PIETRO DA CORTONA   1596–1669
8   Neptune Quieting the Winds
Pen and wash over red chalk. 255 x 350 mm. 10 x 13¾ in.
The Leonora Hall Gurley Memorial Collection   22.494

GIOVANNI BENEDETTO CASTIGLIONE   1616–1670
9   Studies of Animals
Pen and ink over black chalk. 297 x 205 mm. 11⅝ x 8 in.
The David Adler Collection   50.1408

FERDINANDO GALLI BIBIENA 1657–1743

10 Monumental Vestibule
verso: Studies of Arches
Pen and water color. 277 x 187 mm. 10⅞ x 7⅜ in.
The Joseph and Helen Regenstein Collection 59.185

DONATO CRETI 1671–1749

11 The Astronomers
Pen and wash. 240 x 325 mm. 9½ x 12¾ in.
The Worcester Sketch Collection Fund 62.791

ALESSANDRO MAGNASCO 1667–1749

12 Ballad Singer with Shrine of the Virgin
Brown wash with touches of white over black chalk on grey paper
465 x 370 mm. 18⅜ x 14½ in.
The Joseph and Helen Regenstein Collection 62.585

13 Picaresque Group with Monkey and Magpie
Brown wash with touches of white over black chalk on grey paper
477 x 370 mm. 18¾ x 14½ in.
The Joseph and Helen Regenstein Collection 62.586

GIOVANNI BATTISTA TIEPOLO 1696–1770

14 The Meeting of Abraham and Melchizedek
Pen and wash in brown ink over black chalk. 370 x 510 mm. 14½ x 20 in.
Given in Memory of Carl O. Schniewind 58.554

15 Turbaned Head
Red and white chalk on blue paper. 276 x 210 mm. 10⅞ x 8¼ in.
The Simeon B. Williams Fund 42.453

16 The Death of Seneca (Pl. IX)
Pen and wash in brown ink over graphite. 340 x 240 mm. 13⅜ x 9⅜ in.
The Joseph and Helen Regenstein Collection 59.36

ANTONIO CANAL called CANALETTO 1697–1768

17 Ruins of a Courtyard (Pl. VIII)
Pen with brown ink, grey wash over graphite. 293 x 207 mm. 11½ x 8⅛ in.
The Samuel P. Avery Fund 43.514

GIOVANNI ANTONIO GUARDI 1698–1760

18 Il Ridotto (The Masked Ball)
Pen and wash over graphite. 295 x 515 mm. 11⅝ x 20¼ in.
Gift of Tiffany and Margaret Blake 44.579

FRANCESCO ZUCCARELLI 1702–1788

19 Portrait of an Old Man
Black and white chalk on blue-grey paper. 200 x 165 mm. 7⅞ x 6½ in.
The Joseph and Helen Regenstein Collection 60.560

FRANCESCO GUARDI 1712–1793
20   The Adoration of the Shepherds
verso: Three Landscape Studies
Pen and wash in brown ink. 383 x 517 mm. 15⅛ x 20⅜ in.
The Clarence Buckingham Collection 61.48

GIOVANNI BATTISTA PIRANESI 1720–1778
21   Six Figure Studies   (Pl. VI b)
Pen with dark grey ink. 230 x 365 mm. 9 x 14⅜ in.
Gift of Tiffany and Margaret Blake 59.3

22   Fantasy of a Palace with a Fountain at the Right   (Pl. VI a)
Pen and wash in brown ink. 260 x 390 mm. 10¼ x 15⅜ in.
The Ada Turnbull Hertle Fund 63.139

GIOVANNI DOMENICO TIEPOLO 1727–1804
23   Jesus in the House of Jairus   (Pl. VII)
Pen with grey ink, grey and brown wash over black chalk
480 x 382 mm. 18⅞ x 15 in.
Gift of Tiffany and Margaret Blake 60.547

24   Pulchinello Chopping Logs
Pen and wash in brown ink over graphite. 345 x 470 mm. 13½ x 18½ in.
Gift of Emily Crane Chadbourne 57.309

UBALDO GANDOLFI 1728–1781
25   Study for a Ceiling Fresco
Pen and wash over graphite. 335 x 305 mm. 13¼ x 12⅛ in.
The Leonora Hall Gurley Memorial Collection 22.3340

Netherlands before 1800

DIRK VELLERT   active 1511–1544
26   The Triumph of Time   (Pl. X)
Pen and ink. 220 mm. 8⅝ in. diameter
Gift of Potter Palmer 39.261

JACQUES DE GHEYN 1565–1629
27   Three Gypsies   (Pl. XI)
Pen and dark brown ink. 225 x 258 mm. 8⅞ x 10⅛ in.
Gift of Tiffany and Margaret Blake 59.2

SIMON DE VLIEGER 1600–1653
28   Fishermen Drying Nets on Scheveningen Beach
Black and white chalk on tan paper. 280 x 440 mm. 11 x 17¼ in.
Gift of Mr. and Mrs. James W. Alsdorf 60.27

REMBRANDT VAN RIJN 1606–1669

29 Cottage beside a Canal
Pen and wash. 150 x 248 mm. 5⅞ x 9¾ in.
The Clarence Buckingham Collection 53.37

30 Kostverloren Castle in Ruins (Pl. XIII a)
Pen and wash with touches of white. 110 x 175 mm. 4¼ x 6⅞ in.
The Clarence Buckingham Collection 61.49

31 Study of a Female Nude (Pl. XII)
Pen and wash. 233 x 178 mm. 9⅛ x 7⅛ in.
Gift of Tiffany and Margaret Blake 47.464

32 Nude Woman Seated on a Stool
Pen and wash. 210 x 175 mm. 8¼ x 6⅞ in.
The Clarence Buckingham Collection 53.38

33 Noah's Ark (Pl. XIII b)
Reed pen and wash. 200 x 243 mm. 7⅞ x 9½ in.
The Clarence Buckingham Collection 53.36

France before 1900

DANIEL DUMONSTIER (DUMOUSTIER) 1574–1646
34 Portrait of Cardinal de la Rochefoucault "1624" (Pl. XIV)
Red and black chalk with touches of white. 435 x 338 mm. 17⅛ x 13⅜ in.
The Joseph and Helen Regenstein Collection 59.35

JACQUES CALLOT 1592–1635
35 View of the Castello Bracciano
Pen and brown ink. 283 x 910 mm. 11⅛ x 35⅞ in.
The Clarence Buckingham Collection 62.365

36 Sketches of Dancers
Red chalk. 210 x 287 mm. 8¼ x 11¼ in.
Gift of the Print and Drawing Club 40.59

CLAUDE GELLEE called LE LORRAIN 1600–1682
37 Two Ships (Pl. XV)
Pen and wash over black chalk. 317 x 223 mm. 12½ x 8¾ in.
The Worcester Sketch Collection Fund 47.75

38 Study of Trees
White gouache over black chalk on tan paper. 390 x 230 mm. 15⅜ x 9⅛ in.
The Frances A. Elkins Memorial Fund 56.1218

CHARLES LE BRUN 1619–1690
39 The Dead Christ
Pen and wash over traces of red chalk on blue paper. 225 x 350 mm. 8⅞ x 13¾ in.
The Clarence Buckingham Collection 62.375

JEAN JOUVENET 1644–1717
40   The Family of St. John
Black and white chalk and estompe on blue paper. 520 x 300 mm. 20½ x 11⅞ in.
The Worcester Sketch Collection Fund   62.792

JEAN-ANTOINE WATTEAU 1684–1721
41   Spring
Red chalk. 155 x 215 mm. 6⅛ x 8½ in.
Gift of Tiffany and Margaret Blake   55.1004

42   Four Studies of Italian Actors   (Pl. XVII)
Red, black and white chalk on grey paper. 260 x 400 mm. 10¼ x 15¾ in.
Gift of Tiffany and Margaret Blake   54.1

43   Three Studies of a Seated Woman   (Pl. XVI)
Red, black and white chalk on grey paper. 260 x 370 mm. 10¼ x 14⅝ in.
The Joseph and Helen Regenstein Collection   58.8

NICOLAS LANCRET 1690–1743
44   Head of a Young Man
Red, black and white chalk on tan paper. 123 x 105 mm. 4⅞ x 4⅛ in.
The Joseph and Helen Regenstein Collection   60.559

HUBERT GRAVELOT 1699–1773
45   Two studies, of 16, illustrating *Partie de Chasse de Henri IV* by Charles Collé
(The quarto edition was never published although six plates were engraved.)
a. First study for Act III, Scene II
Black chalk. 180 x 150 mm. 7 x 6 in. (oval)
b. Second study for the same subject
Pen and ink over black chalk. 180 x 150 mm. 7 x 6 in. (oval)
Gift of Mr. and Mrs. Louis H. Silver   60.853

JEAN-BAPTISTE-SIMEON CHARDIN 1699–1779
46   Portrait of Françoise-Marguerite Pouget (Mme Chardin)   (Pl. XXIII)
Pastel. 458 x 380 mm. 18 x 15 in.
The Joseph and Helen Regenstein Collection   62.137

FRANÇOIS BOUCHER 1703–1770
47   Valet with a Coffee Pot   (Study for "Le Déjeuner en Famille", 1739)
Red, black and white chalk and graphite. 345 x 195 mm. 13⅝ x 7⅝ in.
The Joseph and Helen Regenstein Collection   59.183

48   Boy Fishing   (Pl. XVIII)
Black and white chalk on blue paper
300 x 443 mm. 11⅞ x 17½ in.
The Joseph and Helen Regenstein Collection   60.206

49   Venus and Amor
Pen and wash in rose and brown ink over traces of black chalk
248 x 315 mm. (oval) 9¾ x 12½ in.
The Joseph and Helen Regenstein Collection   60.557

MAURICE-QUENTIN DE LA TOUR 1704–1788

50   Self-Portrait   (Pl. XXII)
Pastel on pale green paper. 325 x 240 mm. 12¾ x 9½ in.
The Joseph and Helen Regenstein Collection   59.242

51   Portrait of M. Louis de Silvestre
Black and white chalk on green paper with touches of red and blue
300 x 250 mm. 11¾ x 7⅞ in.
The Joseph and Helen Regenstein Collection   58.543

LOUIS CARROGIS DE CARMONTELLE 1717–1806

52   Countess Cossée
Black and red chalk and water color. 310 x 200 mm. 12¼ x 7⅞ in.
Gift of Robert Allerton   56.58

GABRIEL-JACQUES DE SAINT-AUBIN 1724–1780

53   Four Studies of a Young Girl
Black chalk and graphite. 167 x 220 mm. 6⅝ x 8⅝ in.
The David Adler Collection   44.592

54   Sketchbook   ca. 1760–64
Pen and brown ink, black chalk and water color
172 x 130 mm. 6¾ x 5⅛ in.
Gift of Herman Waldeck   46.383

55   Allegory of Vanity   "1767"
Pen, water color over black chalk. 190 x 130 mm. 7½ x 5⅛ in.
Gift of Tiffany and Margaret Blake   61.34

JEAN-BAPTISTE GREUZE 1725–1805

56   The Return of the Prodigal Son
Pen and wash over black chalk. 370 x 505 mm. 14⅝ x 20 in.
Gift of Mr. and Mrs. Leigh B. Block   55.1003

JEAN-HONORE FRAGONARD 1732–1806

57   Arbor with two Children (Le Nid d'Amour)   "1760"   (Pl. XIX)
Red chalk. 360 x 485 mm. 14⅛ x 19⅛ in.
The Joseph and Helen Regenstein Collection   62.486

58   A Bull of the Roman Campagna
Wash over graphite. 363 x 493 mm. 14¼ x 19⅜ in.
The Joseph and Helen Regenstein Collection   62.116

59   Portrait of Mlle Vignier   "1774"   (Pl. XXI)
Wash over graphite. 427 x 327 mm. 16¾ x 12⅞ in.
The Joseph and Helen Regenstein Collection   60.209

60   The Letter (The Spanish Conversation)   (Pl. XX)
Wash over graphite. 397 x 290 mm. 15⅝ x 11⅜ in.
Gift of Tiffany and Margaret Blake   45.32

61   Portrait of Benjamin Franklin.   1778
Wash. 278 x 238 mm. 10⅞ x 9⅜ in.
Given in Memory of Charles Netcher II   33.806

HUBERT ROBERT 1733–1808

62   Round Fountain in a Roman Garden
Red chalk. 307 x 435 mm. 12⅛ x 17⅛ in.
Gift of Tiffany and Margaret Blake   62.810

CLAUDE MICHEL called CLODION 1738–1814

63   Two Fauns Supporting an Urn
Red chalk. 315 x 450 mm. 12⅜ x 18⅛ in.
The Worcester Sketch Collection Fund   62.352

JEAN-MICHEL MOREAU called MOREAU LE JEUNE 1741–1814

64   The Young Godparents
Wash over black chalk. 225 x 170 mm. 8⅞ x 6⅝ in.
The Joseph and Helen Regenstein Collection   60.825

JACQUES-LOUIS DAVID 1748–1825

65   Study for "The Oath of the Tennis Court"   (Pl. XXVII)
Pencil, pen and wash. 390 x 255 mm. 15½ x 10 in.
The Joseph and Helen Regenstein Collection   60.207

66   Profile Portrait of an Old Man (Prieur de la Marne?)
Black chalk. 230 x 230 mm. 9 x 9 in.
The Joseph and Helen Regenstein Collection   60.196

67   Sketchbook containing a series of studies for "The Distribution of the Eagles"   1810
Pencil, occasionally pen. 242 x 190 mm. 9½ x 7½ in.
The Joseph and Helen Regenstein Collection   61.393

68   Studies of Men from the Sketchbook: Cambacérès and Lebrun (top left);
Napoléon (top center); others unidentified
Pencil. 242 x 190 mm. 9½ x 7½ in.
The Joseph and Helen Regenstein Collection   61.393

69   Studies of Men from the Sketchbook: Portrait of Prince Eugène de
Beauharnais (above); Heads of Models (below)
Pencil, black chalk, pen and ink. 242 x 190 mm. 9½ x 7½ in.
The Joseph and Helen Regenstein Collection   61.393

70   Studies of Women from the Sketchbook: Baronne Meunier (left);
Caroline Bonaparte, Queen of Naples (center); Mme Mongez [?] (right)
Pencil. 242 x 190 mm. 9½ x 7½ in.
The Joseph and Helen Regenstein Collection   61.393

CLAUDE HOIN 1750–1817

71   Portrait of a Young Man
Black and white chalk and estompe on tan paper
385 x 277 mm. 15⅛ x 10⅞ in.
Anonymous Gift   60.197

LOUIS-PHILIBERT DEBUCOURT 1755–1832

72   The Dressing Room of the Extras of the Comédie Française
Grey and black wash over black chalk. 333 x 447 mm. 13⅛ x 17⅝ in.
The Joseph and Helen Regenstein Collection   60.208

PIERRE-PAUL PRUD'HON 1758–1823

73   Head of Vengeance (Study for "Justice and Vengeance Pursuing Crime" 1808)
Black and white chalk and estompe on blue paper. 510 x 395 mm. 20 x 15½ in.
The Arthur Heun Fund 52.1111   (Pl. XXVI)

74   Minerva, Poet Laureate and Other Studies
verso: Embracing Genii
Chinese white and brown wash over graphite on blue paper
290 x 442 mm. 11⅜ x 17⅜ in.
Print and Drawing Department Purchase Fund 56.57

JEAN-AUGUSTE-DOMINIQUE INGRES 1780–1867

75   Charles-François Mallet, Civil Engineer "1809"
Pencil. 268 x 210 mm. 10½ x 8¼ in.
The Charles Deering Collection 38.166

76   Doctor Robin (Pl. XXXI)
Pencil. 285 x 222 mm. 11¼ x 8¾ in.
Gift of Emily Crane Chadbourne 53.204

77   View of St. Peter's in Rome (Pl. XXXIII)
Pencil. 330 x 490 mm. 13 x 19¼ in.
The Joseph and Helen Regenstein Collection 61.31

78   Charles X in His Coronation Robes ca. 1828
Water color over pencil. 263 x 200 mm. 10¼ x 7⅞ in.
The Worcester Sketch Collection Fund 60.352

79   Pierre-Alexandre Tardieu, the Engraver
Pencil. 242 x 185 mm. 9½ x 7¼ in.
The David Adler Collection 50.1513

THEODORE GERICAULT 1791–1824

80   General of the First Empire Giving His Cavalry Orders to Charge
Water color over pencil and red pencil. 535 x 450 mm. 21 x 17¾ in.
The Ada Turnbull Hertle Fund. 60.8   (Pl. XXVIII)

81   Study for the lithograph "Return from Russia" ca. 1818
(Sheet 7 recto from the album)   (Pl. XXIX)
Pencil. 225 x 288 mm. 8¾ x 11¼ in.
Gift of Tiffany and Margaret Blake 47.35

82   Study for the lithograph "The Boxers" ca. 1818
(Sheet 15 recto from the album)
Pencil. 218 x 282 mm. 8½ x 11 in.
Gift of Tiffany and Margaret Blake 47.35

83   Stableboy Grooming a Horse ca. 1818–1820
(Sheet 27 recto from the album)
Pencil and wash. 275 x 210 mm. 10¾ x 8¼ in.
Gift of Tiffany and Margaret Blake 47.35

84   Five Sketches for a Cavalry Battle ca. 1814
(Sheet 50 recto from the album)
Pencil, pen and ink. 183 x 228 mm. 6¾ x 9 in.
Gift of Tiffany and Margaret Blake 47.35

JEAN-BAPTISTE-CAMILLE COROT 1796–1875
85   View of Nepi   "1826"   (Pl. XXXII)
Pencil. 223 x 350 mm. 8¾ x 13¾ in.
The Arthur Heun Fund   53.529

FERDINAND-VICTOR-EUGENE DELACROIX 1798–1863
86   Four Studies of Arabs   1832
Pencil and water color. 183 x 268 mm. 7¼ x 10½ in.
Given in Memory of Her Husband by Mrs. Francis H. Hardy   60.822

87   Studies of Arms and Legs, after "The Crucifixion" by Rubens
in Antwerp   (Pl. XXXVI)
Pen and brush in brown ink. 215 x 322 mm. 8½ x 12¾ in.
The Worcester Sketch Collection Fund   62.353

HONORE DAUMIER 1808–1879
88   A Group of Men and Other Studies   (Pl. XXXIV)
Pencil. 420 x 303 mm. 16½ x 12 in.
Given in Memory of Tiffany Blake   48.19

89   Fatherly Discipline   (Pl. XXXV)
Pen and grey wash over charcoal. 253 x 200 mm. 10 x 7⅞ in.
The Arthur Heun Fund   52.1108

90   Fright
Charcoal over pencil. 210 x 240 mm. 8¼ x 9⅜ in.
Gift of Robert Allerton   23.944

JEAN-FRANÇOIS MILLET 1814–1875
91   Female Nude
Black chalk. 270 x 197 mm. 10⅝ x 7¾ in.
The Edward E. Ayer Fund   52.61

CHARLES-FRANÇOIS DAUBIGNY 1817–1878
92   Landscape with a Rainbow
Red and black chalk. 310 x 485 mm. 12⅛ x 19⅛ in.
Gift of Mr. and Mrs. Leigh B. Block   62.377

THEODORE CHASSERIAU 1819–1856
93   Baroness Frédéric Chassériau   "1846"   (Pl. XXX)
Pencil. 313 x 235 mm. 12¼ x 9¼ in.
The David Adler Collection   50.1904

PIERRE PUVIS DE CHAVANNES 1824–1898
94   The Fisherman's Family   1887
Red chalk. 308 x 250 mm. 12⅛ x 9⅞ in.
Gift of Robert Allerton   24.928

JEAN-BAPTISTE CARPEAUX 1827–1875
95   Study for Ugolino   "1860"   (Pl. XXXVII)
Grey and white gouache, pen and brown ink. 622 x 480 mm. 24½ x 18⅞ in.
The Joseph and Helen Regenstein Collection   63.264

GUSTAVE DORE 1832–1883

96 Three Giants Captured by a Knight
Water color, pen and ink. 445 x 365 mm. 17½ x 14¾ in.
The Olivia Shaler Swan Memorial Fund 63.32

EDOUARD MANET 1832–1883

97 Full Length Figure of a Boy (Léon Leenhoff) ca. 1865 (Pl. XLI)
Conté crayon. 405 x 205 mm. 16 x 8⅛ in.
The Joseph and Helen Regenstein Collection 63.140

98 Page with Five Marine Scenes ca. 1871
Water color and pencil. 325 x 260 mm. 12¾ x 10¼ in.
Bequest of Grant J. Pick

99 La Rue Mosnier ca. 1878
Pencil and brush with India ink. 278 x 440 mm. 10⅞ x 17⅜ in.
Given in Memory of Tiffany Blake 45.15

EDGAR DEGAS 1834–1917

100 Portrait of René de Gas ca. 1855 (Pl. XXXVIII)
Black chalk. 347 x 275 mm. 13⅝ x 10¾ in.
The Joseph and Helen Regenstein Collection 61.792

101 Italian Head ca. 1856
Charcoal with estompe. 380 x 260 mm. 15 x 10¼ in.
Gift of Tiffany and Margaret Blake 45.37

102 Mme Michel Musson and Her Two Daughters "1865" (Pl. XXXIX)
Pencil, grey and brown wash with touches of Chinese white
350 x 265 mm. 13¾ x 10⅜ in.
Gift of Tiffany and Margaret Blake 49.20

103 Four Studies of a Jockey ca. 1866
Brush with oil. 450 x 305 mm. 17⅝ x 12 in.
Mr. and Mrs. Lewis L. Coburn Memorial Collection 33.469

104 Ballet Dancer Bending Forward ca. 1885
Charcoal, white and yellow chalk on blue paper. 460 x 305 mm. 18⅛ x 12 in.
Mr. and Mrs. Martin A. Ryerson Collection 33.1230

105 After the Bath: Woman Drying Her Feet ca. 1890
Charcoal with touches of pastel. 570 x 408 mm. 22⅜ x 16 in.
Gift of Mrs. Potter Palmer 45.34

HENRI FANTIN-LATOUR 1836–1904

106 Portrait of Ingres "1865"
Charcoal and estompe. 162 x 110 mm. 6⅜ x 4¼ in.
Gift of Emily Crane Chadbourne 28.166

PAUL CEZANNE 1839–1906

107 Study for "The Autopsy" ca. 1867–69
Charcoal. 310 x 485 mm. 12¼ x 19⅛ in.
Gift of Tiffany and Margaret Blake 47.36

108   Harlequin (Study for "Mardi Gras" of 1888)   (Pl. XL)
Pencil. 473 x 310 mm. 18⅝ x 12¼ in.
Gift of Tiffany and Margaret Blake   44.577

109   Sketchbook   ca. 1868–75
Pencil, occasionally pen and ink. 125 x 223 mm. 5 x 8¾ in.
The Arthur Heun Fund   51.1

110   Pistachio Tree at Château Noir   ca. 1895–1900
Water color and pencil. 540 x 430 mm. 21¼ x 17 in.
Mr. and Mrs. Martin A. Ryerson Collection   37.1030

ODILON REDON   1840–1916
111   Winged Head above the Water
Charcoal. 465 x 372 mm. 18¼ x 14⅝ in.
The David Adler Collection   50.1428

BERTHE MORISOT   1841–1895
112   On the Balcony   1872
Water color over pencil sketch. 205 x 175 mm. 8⅛ x 6⅞ in.
Given in Memory of Charles Netcher II   33.1

PIERRE-AUGUSTE RENOIR   1841–1919
113   Study for "The Bathers"   1884–85   (Pl. XLIII)
Pencil, red, black and white chalk touched with brush
985 x 640 mm. 38¾ x 25¼ in.
Bequest of Kate L. Brewster   49.514

PAUL GAUGUIN   1848–1903
114   Woman Bather in Brittany   1886–87   (Pl. XLII)
Black chalk and pastel. 585 x 350 mm. 23 x 13¾ in.
Given in Memory of Charles B. Goodspeed by Mrs. Gilbert W. Chapman   46.292

115   Crouching Tahitian Girl   1891–2   (Pl. XLV)
Pencil, charcoal and pastel. 553 x 478 mm. 21¾ x 18⅞ in.
Gift of Tiffany and Margaret Blake   44.578

116   Head of a Tahitian Man   1891–3
Black and red chalk over pencil. 350 x 387 mm. 13¾ x 15¼ in.
Gift of Emily Crane Chadbourne   22.4794

GEORGES SEURAT   1859–1891
117   Lady with a Muff   ca. 1884   (Pl. XLVII)
Conté crayon. 313 x 238 mm. 12¼ x 9⅜ in.
Gift of Robert Allerton   26.716

HENRI DE TOULOUSE-LAUTREC   1864–1901
118   Sketchbook   1880
Pencil, black grease crayon and occasionally pen and ink and water color
160 x 257 mm. 6¼ x 10⅛ in.
The Robert Alexander Waller Memorial Fund   49.80

119   The Cortege of the Rajah   1895   (Pl. XLVI)
Black crayon and blue pencil. 440 x 325 mm. 17¼ x 12⅞ in.
The Worcester Sketch Collection Fund   59.81

120   At the Circus: Trained Pony and Baboon   1899
Pencil, colored crayon and estompe. 440 x 267 mm. 17¼ x 10½ in.
Gift of Tiffany and Margaret Blake   44.581

Spain before 1900

FRANCISCO JOSE GOYA Y LUCIENTES   1746–1828
121   Cuydado con ese paso (Be Careful with that Step)   (Pl. XXIV)
Grey and black wash. 263 x 182 mm. 10⅜ x 7⅛ in.
The Joseph and Helen Regenstein Collection   58.542

122   Sueño de azotes (Dream of Flogging)   (Pl. XXV)
Grey and black wash. 233 x 142 mm. 9⅛ x 5⅝ in.
The Clarence Buckingham Collection   61.785

123   Three Men Carrying a Wounded One
Brown wash. 205 x 140 mm. 8 x 5½ in.
The Clarence Buckingham Collection   60.313

England before 1900

GEORGE ROMNEY   1734–1802
124   Lady Hamilton as Ariadne
Brown wash. 423 x 238 mm. 17 x 9⅜ in.
Gift of Tiffany and Margaret Blake   44.580

HENRY FUSELI   1741–1825
125   The Cave of Despayre
(Book I, Canto IX of Edmund Spenser's *The Faerie Queen*)
Pen and water color over graphite. 330 x 495 mm. 13 x 19½ in.
The Leonora Hall Gurley Memorial Collection   22.2151

AUGUSTUS PUGIN   1762–1832
126   The Chancel of Temple Church
(Preparatory drawing for Plate 84 of *The Microcosm of London*)
Pencil, pen and wash. 318 x 202 mm. 12½ x 8 in.
The Charles Deering Collection   40.1059

JOSEPH MALLORD WILLIAM TURNER   1775–1851
127   Bampton Grange
Pencil. 285 x 428 mm. 11⅛ x 16⅞ in.
The Leonora Hall Gurley Memorial Collection   22.1469

128 View of Lucerne
Water color with areas of the paper scratched away
230 x 290 mm. 9⅛ x 11⅜ in.
Given by Margaret Mower in Memory of her mother Elsa Durand Mower 60.10

JOHN RUSKIN 1819–1900

129 Landscape Study
Pencil, pen, brown ink and water color. 320 x 455 mm. 12⅝ x 17⅞ in.
The Charles Deering Collection 27.6405

Belgium & Holland 19th & 20th Centuries

VINCENT VAN GOGH 1853–1890

130 Despair (Pl. XLIV)
Black chalk with touches of white chalk and ink wash
500 x 310 mm. 19⅝ x 12¼ in.
Given in Memory of Tiffany Blake 47.23

131 Tree in a Meadow 1889
Reed pen and ink over traces of black chalk or charcoal
492 x 613 mm. 19⅜ x 24⅛ in.
Gift of Tiffany and Margaret Blake 45.31

132 Grove of Cypresses 1889
Reed pen and ink over pencil. 625 x 465 mm. 24⅝ x 18¼ in.
Gift of Robert Allerton 27.543

JAMES ENSOR 1860–1949

133 The Death of Jezebel "1880"
Charcoal. 700 x 505 mm. 27½ x 20 in.
Gift of Tiffany and Margaret Blake 60.156

THEO (THEOPHILE) VAN RYSSELBERGHE 1862–1926

134 Marie Sèthe (Mme Henry Van de Velde) at the Piano 1891
Conté crayon. 317 x 358 mm. 12½ x 14⅛ in.
The John H. Wrenn Memorial Collection 55.638

PIET MONDRIAN 1872–1944

135 Trees by the River Gein before 1908
Charcoal. 468 x 623 mm. 18⅜ x 24½ in.
The Edward E. Ayer Fund 62.105

United States 19th & 20th Centuries

WINSLOW HOMER 1836–1910

136 Marblehead "1880"
Water color. 225 x 340 mm. 8⅞ x 13⅜ in.
Mr. and Mrs. Martin A. Ryerson Collection 33.1244

137 Prout's Neck, Breaking Wave "1887"
Water color. 385 x 547 mm. 15⅛ x 21½ in.
Mr. and Mrs. Martin A. Ryerson Collection 33.1248

MAURICE PRENDERGAST 1861–1924
138   The Mall, Central Park   "1901"
Water color. 388 x 570 mm. 15¼ x 22½ in.
The Olivia Shaler Swan Memorial Fund   39.431

GEORGE BELLOWS 1882–1925
139   Study for "Portrait of My Mother"   1920
Black grease crayon. 500 x 312 mm. 19¾ x 12¼ in.
Gift of The Friends of American Art   22.5556

CHARLES SHEELER 1883
140   New York   "1920"
Pencil. 550 x 390 mm. 21⅝ x 15⅜ in.
Gift of The Friends of American Art   22.5552

Germany   20th Century

LOVIS CORINTH 1858–1925
141   Portrait of Goeritz and His Wife   "1922"
Water color. 610 x 485 mm. 24 x 19⅛ in.
The Worcester Sketch Collection Fund   61.349

KATHE KOLLWITZ 1867–1945
142   Bust of a Woman   "1902"
Black chalk with touches of white and pale tan chalk
405 x 320 mm. 16 x 12⅝ in.
The Herman Waldeck Memorial Fund   60.362

PAUL KLEE 1879–1940
143   Hungernde Geister (Starving Spirits)   "1934"
Pastel and oil on cloth. 510 x 430 mm. 20 x 17 in.
Gift of Tiffany and Margaret Blake   48.15

ERNST LUDWIG KIRCHNER 1880–1938
144   Two Nudes   "1905"
Colored chalk. 645 x 900 mm. 25¼ x 35⅜ in.
The Albert Kunstadter Family Fund

MAX BECKMANN 1884–1950
145   Carnival in Naples   "1944"   (Pl. LIV)
Brush with India ink, black crayon and white chalk on brown paper
1,105 x 695 mm. 39½ x 27⅜ in.
Gift of Tiffany and Margaret Blake   48.5

OSKAR KOKOSCHKA 1886–
146   Portrait of a Woman   "1916"
Black grease crayon. 680 x 470 mm. 26¾ x 18½ in.
Gift of Tiffany and Margaret Blake   46.430

School of Paris 20th Century

EMILE-ANTOINE BOURDELLE 1861–1929
147   Study for the Head of Beethoven
Pen and ink. 233 x 208 mm. 9⅛ x 8¼ in.
Gift of Mme Emile-Antoine Bourdelle   62.778

ARISTIDE MAILLOL 1861–1944
148   Reclining Nude
Red chalk, traces of charcoal. 540 x 780 mm. 21¼ x 30¾ in.
Gift of Mr. and Mrs. William N. Eisendrath, Jr.   40.1044

EDOUARD VUILLARD 1867–1940
149   The Game of Checkers
Pastel. 375 x 305 mm. 14¾ x 12 in.
Gift of Mr. and Mrs. Leigh B. Block   56.35

PIERRE BONNARD 1867–1947
150   Still Life: Preparation for Lunch   1940
Gouache. 500 x 650 mm. 19⅝ x 25⅝ in.
The Olivia Shaler Swan Memorial Fund   43.89

HENRI MATISSE 1869–1954
151   Nude in Armchair   ca. 1906
Brush with India ink. 658 x 465 mm. 25⅞ x 18⅜ in.
Gift of Mrs. Potter Palmer   44.576

JACQUES VILLON 1875–1963
152   Les Vingt Ans Fiers   1930
Gouache, pen and ink. 270 x 208 mm. 10⅝ x 8¼ in.
Gift of Frank B. Hubachek   60.354

ANDRE DERAIN 1880–1954
153   Bust of a Woman
Red chalk. 605 x 493 mm. 23⅞ x 19⅜ in.
Gift of Mr. and Mrs. William N. Eisendrath, Jr.   40.1045

PABLO PICASSO 1881
154   Fernande Olivier   1906   (Pl. XLIX)
Charcoal. 612 x 458 mm. 24⅛ x 18 in.
Gift of Herman Waldeck   51.210

155   Peasant Girls from Andorra   1906   (Pl. XLVIII)
Pen and ink. 633 x 433 mm. 25 x 17 in.
Gift of Robert Allerton   30.933

156   Woman Washing Her Feet   "1944"
Pencil. 505 x 383 mm. 19⅞ x 15⅛ in.
Bequest of Curt Valentin   55.603

GINO SEVERINI 1883
157 Train Crossing a Street
Charcoal. 555 x 465 mm. 21⅞ x 18¼ in.
The Alfred Stieglitz Collection 49.903

AMEDEO MODIGLIANI 1884–1920
158 Seated Nude 1918 (Pl. L)
Pencil. 425 x 250 mm. 16¾ x 9⅞ in.
Given in Memory of Tiffany Blake by Claire Swift von der Marwitz 51.22

JULES PASCIN 1885–1930
159 Seated Man (Pl. LII)
verso: Woman at Table
Pen and ink. 635 x 480 mm. 25 x 19 in.
Given in Memory of Mary McDonald Ludgin 63.30

ROGER DE LA FRESNAYE 1885–1925
160 Classic Head "1924"
Red chalk. 270 x 210 mm. 10⅝ x 8¼ in.
Gift of Mrs. Potter Palmer 45.35

JUAN GRIS 1887–1927
161 Still Life with a Siphon "1917" (Pl. LI)
Charcoal. 470 x 312 mm. 18½ x 12¼ in.
Gift of Mr. and Mrs. Leigh B. Block 54.1061

GIORGIO DE CHIRICO 1888
162 Autumnal Still Life "1917"
Pencil. 300 x 222 mm. 11⅞ x 8¾ in.
The William Mc Callin Mc Kee Memorial Collection 44.585

MARC CHAGALL 1889
163 The Angel and the Reader
Gouache. 635 x 490 mm. 25 x 19¼ in.
The Olivia Shaler Swan Memorial Fund 41.829

JOAN MIRO 1893
164 Persons Haunted by a Bird 1938
Water color over black and brown chalk. 410 x 330 mm. 16¼ x 13 in.
Gift of Mr. and Mrs. Peter B. Bensinger 60.327

PAVEL TCHELITCHEW 1898–1957
165 Portrait of Gertrude Stein "1930" (Pl. LIII)
Brush with India ink. 425 x 288 mm. 16¾ x 11⅜ in.
Given in Memory of Charles B. Goodspeed by Mrs. Gilbert W. Chapman 47.792

Pl. I   1. Anonymous North Italian: Portrait of a Young Priest

Pl. II   4. Carpaccio: Standing Youth

Pl. III   2. Pisanello: Studies of the Patriarch of Constantinople

Pl. IV 7. Palma Giovane: The Entombment

Pl. V   6. Veronese: Studies for a Descent from the Cross

Pl. VIa   22. Piranesi: Fantasy of a Palace

Pl. VIb   21. Piranesi: Six Figure Studies

Pl. VII   23. Giovanni Domenico Tiepolo: Jesus in the House of Jairus

Pl. VIII   17. Canaletto: Ruins of a Courtyard

Pl. IX   16. Giovanni Battista Tiepolo: Death of Seneca

Pl. X   26. Dirk Vellert: The Triumph of Time

Pl. XI   27. Jacques de Gheyn: Three Gypsies

Pl. XII   31. Rembrandt: Study of a Female Nude

Pl. XIIIa   30. Rembrandt: Kostverloren Castle in Ruins

Pl. XIIIb   33. Rembrandt: Noah's Ark

LE CARDINAL DE LA ROCHEFOUCAULT

1624

Pl. XIV   34. Dumonstier: Cardinal de la Rochefoucault

Pl. XV   37. Claude Gellée: Two Ships

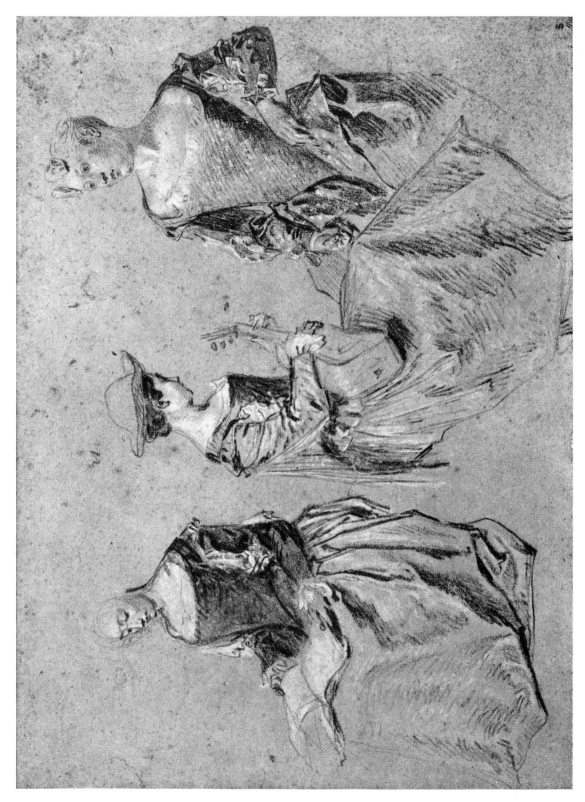

PL. XVI   43. Watteau: Three Studies of a Seated Woman

Pl. XVII   42. Watteau: Four Studies of Italian Actors

Pl. XVIII   48. Boucher: Boy Fishing

Pl. XIX 57. Fragonard: Arbor with Two Children

Pl. XX 60. *Fragonard: The Letter*

Pl. XXI   59. Fragonard: Mlle Vignier

Pl. XXII   50. Maurice-Quentin de La Tour: Self-Portrait

Pl. XXIII   46. Chardin: Mme Chardin

Pl. XXIV 121. Goya: Be Careful with that Step

Pl. XXV   122. Goya: Dream of Flogging

Pl. XXVI   73. Prud'hon: Head of Vengeance

Pl. XXVII   65. David: Study for "The Oath of the Tennis Court"

Pl. XXVIII   80. Géricault: General of the First Empire Giving Orders to Charge

Pl. XXIX 81. Géricault: Return from Russia

Pl. XXX   93. Chassériau: Baroness Frédéric Chassériau

Pl. XXXI   76. Ingres: Doctor Robin

Pl. XXXII 85. Corot: View of Nepi

Pl. XXXIII   77. Ingres: View of St. Peter's in Rome

Pl. XXXIV   88. Daumier: A Group of Men and Other Studies

Pl. XXXV   89. Daumier: Fatherly Discipline

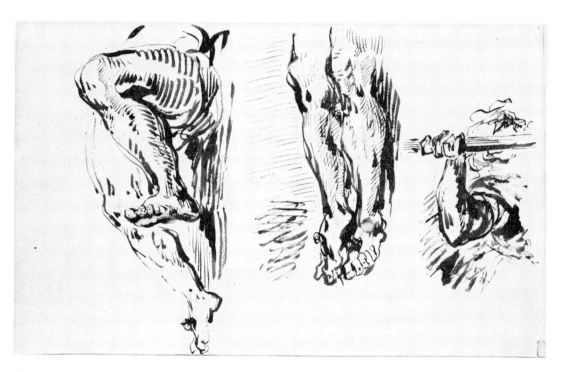

Pl. XXXVI 87. Delacroix: Studies after Rubens' "Crucifixion"

Pl. XXXVII   95. Carpeaux: Study for Ugolino

Pl. XXXVIII   100. Degas: Portrait of René de Gas

Pl. XXXIX   102. Degas: Mme Musson and her Daughters

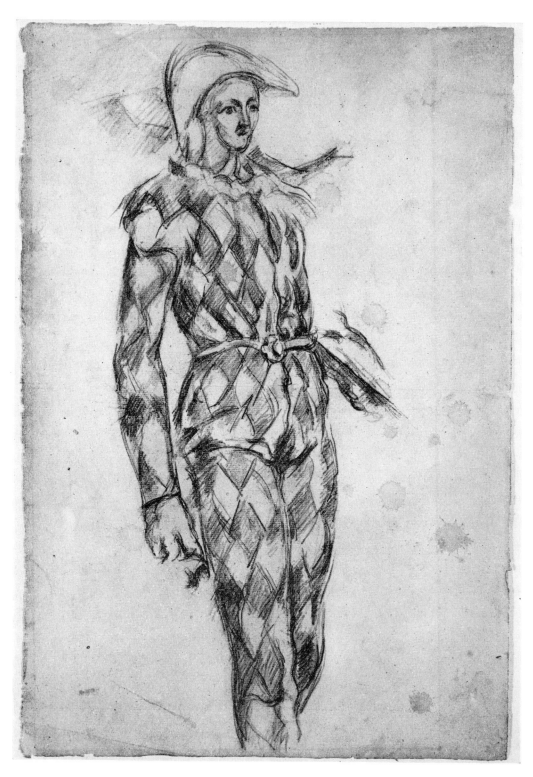

Pl. XL   108. Cézanne: Harlequin

Pl. XLI   97. Manet: Figure of a Boy (Léon Leenhoff)

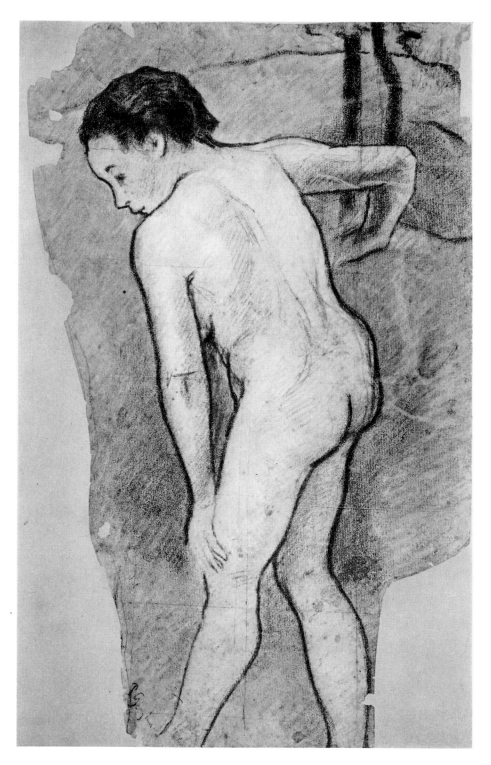

Pl. XLII   114. Gauguin: Woman Bather in Brittany

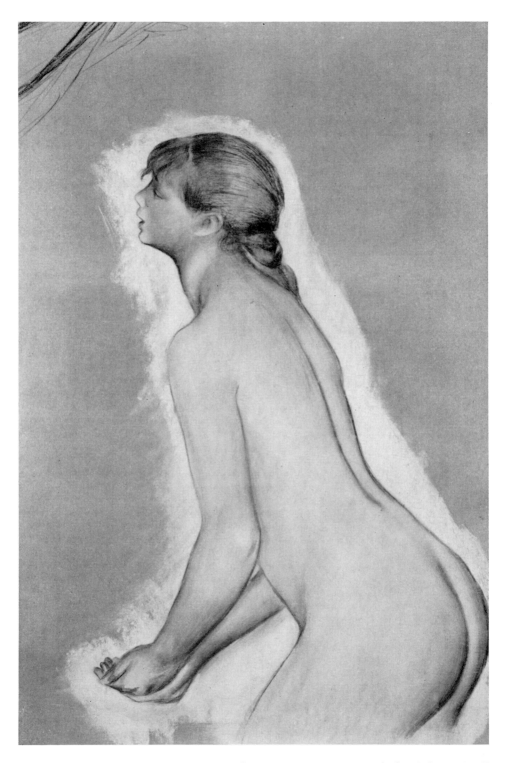

Pl. XLIII   113. Renoir: Study for "The Bathers"

Pl. XLIV   130. Van Gogh: Despair

Pl. XLV 115. Gauguin: Crouching Tahitian Girl

Pl. XLVI   119. Toulouse-Lautrec: The Cortege of the Rajah

Pl. XLVII   117. Seurat: Lady with a Muff

Pl. XLVIII   155. Picasso: Peasant Girls from Andorra

Pl. XLIX   154. Picasso: Fernande Olivier

Pl. L   158. Modigliani: Seated Nude

Pl. LI   161. Juan Gris: Still Life with a Siphon

Pl. LII   159. Pascin: Seated Man

Pl. LIII   165. Tchelitchew: Portrait of Gertrude Stein

Pl. LIV   145. Max Beckmann: Carnival in Naples